All-Time Favorite
Casseroles

Publications International, Ltd.
Favorite Brand Name Recipes at www.fbnr.com

Pictured on the front cover: Creamy Chicken and Pasta with Spinach *(page 40)*.

Pictured on the back cover *(clockwise from top):* Ravioli with Homemade Tomato Sauce *(page 74)*, Chicken Enchiladas *(page 32)* and Spicy Turkey Casserole *(page 34)*.

ISBN: 0-7853-6032-8

Manufactured in China.

8 7 6 5 4 3 2 1

Microwave Cooking: Microwave ovens vary in wattage. Use the cooking times as guidelines and check for doneness before adding more time.

Preparation/Cooking Times: Preparation times are based on the approximate amount of time required to assemble the recipe before cooking, baking, chilling or serving. These times include preparation steps such as measuring, chopping and mixing. The fact that some preparations and cooking can be done simultaneously is taken into account. Preparation of optional ingredients and serving suggestions is not included.

All-Time Favorite Casseroles

pg. 8

pg. 52

pg. 82

Daybreak Delights

Summer Sausage 'n' Egg Wedges

4 eggs, beaten
$\frac{1}{3}$ cup milk
$\frac{1}{4}$ cup all-purpose flour
$\frac{1}{2}$ teaspoon baking powder
$\frac{1}{8}$ teaspoon garlic powder
2$\frac{1}{2}$ cups (10 ounces) shredded Cheddar or mozzarella cheese, divided
1$\frac{1}{2}$ cups diced HILLSHIRE FARM® Summer Sausage
1 cup cream-style cottage cheese with chives

Preheat oven to 375°F.

Combine eggs, milk, flour, baking powder and garlic powder in medium bowl; beat until combined. Stir in 2 cups Cheddar cheese, Summer Sausage and cottage cheese. Pour into greased 9-inch pie plate. Bake, uncovered, 25 to 30 minutes or until golden and knife inserted into center comes out clean. To serve, cut into 6 wedges. Sprinkle wedges with remaining $\frac{1}{2}$ cup Cheddar cheese.

Makes 6 servings

pg. 8

pg. 14

Summer Sausage 'n' Egg Wedge

Low Fat Turkey Bacon Frittata

1 package (12 ounces) BUTTERBALL® Turkey Bacon, heated and chopped
6 ounces uncooked angel hair pasta, broken
2 teaspoons olive oil
1 small onion, sliced
1 red bell pepper, cut into thin strips
4 containers (4 ounces each) egg substitute
1 container (5 ounces) fat free ricotta cheese
1 cup (4 ounces) shredded fat free mozzarella cheese
1 cup (4 ounces) shredded reduced fat Swiss cheese
½ teaspoon salt
½ teaspoon black pepper
1 package (10 ounces) frozen spinach, thawed and squeezed dry

Cook and drain pasta. Heat oil in large skillet over medium heat until hot. Cook and stir onion and bell pepper until tender. Combine egg substitute, cheeses, salt, black pepper and cooked pasta in large bowl. Add vegetables, spinach and turkey bacon. Spray 10-inch quiche dish with nonstick cooking spray; pour mixture into dish. Bake in preheated 350°F oven 30 minutes. Cut into wedges. Serve with spicy salsa, if desired.

Makes 8 servings

Ham & Cheese Grits Soufflé

3 cups water
¾ cup quick-cooking grits
½ teaspoon salt
½ cup (2 ounces) shredded mozzarella cheese
2 ounces ham, finely chopped
2 tablespoons minced chives
2 eggs, separated
Dash hot pepper sauce

1. Preheat oven to 375°F. Grease 1½-quart soufflé dish or deep casserole.

2. Bring water to a boil in medium saucepan. Stir in grits and salt. Cook, stirring frequently, about 5 minutes or until thickened. Stir in cheese, ham, chives, egg yolks and hot pepper sauce.

3. In small clean bowl, beat egg whites until stiff but not dry; fold into grits mixture. Pour into prepared dish. Bake about 30 minutes or until puffed and golden. Serve immediately.

Makes 4 to 6 servings

Low Fat Turkey Bacon Frittata

Cheddar Cheese Strata

1 pound French bread, cut into
    1/2- to 3/4-inch slices, crusts
    removed, divided
2 cups (8 ounces) shredded
    reduced-fat Cheddar
    cheese, divided
2 whole eggs
3 egg whites
1 quart fat-free (skim) milk
1 teaspoon dry mustard
1 teaspoon grated fresh onion
1/2 teaspoon salt
    Paprika to taste

1. Spray 13×9-inch glass baking dish with nonstick cooking spray. Place half the bread slices in bottom of prepared dish, overlapping slightly. Sprinkle with 1 1/4 cups cheese. Place remaining bread slices on top of cheese.

2. Whisk whole eggs and egg whites in large bowl. Add milk, mustard, onion and salt; whisk until well blended. Pour evenly over bread and cheese. Cover with remaining 3/4 cup cheese and sprinkle with paprika. Cover and refrigerate 1 hour or overnight.

3. Preheat oven to 350°F. Bake about 45 minutes or until cheese is melted and bread is golden brown. Let stand 5 minutes before serving. Garnish with red bell pepper stars and fresh Italian parsley, if desired.

Makes 8 servings

Lit'l Links Soufflé

8 slices white bread
2 cups (8 ounces) shredded
    Cheddar cheese
1 pound HILLSHIRE FARM®
    Lit'l Polskas
6 eggs
2 3/4 cups milk
3/4 teaspoon dry mustard

Spread bread in bottom of greased 13×9-inch baking pan. Sprinkle cheese over top of bread.

Arrange Lit'l Polskas on top of cheese. Beat eggs with milk and mustard in large bowl; pour over links. Cover pan with aluminum foil; refrigerate overnight.

Preheat oven to 300°F. Bake egg mixture 1 1/2 hours or until puffy and brown.

Makes 4 to 6 servings

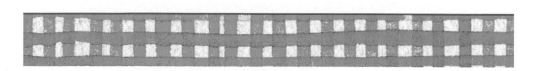

Chiles Rellenos en Casserole

3 eggs, separated
¾ cup milk
¾ cup all-purpose flour
½ teaspoon salt
1 tablespoon butter or margarine
½ cup chopped onion
8 peeled roasted whole chiles *or* 2 cans (7 ounces each) whole green chiles, drained
8 ounces Monterey Jack cheese, cut into 8 strips

CONDIMENTS

Sour cream
Sliced green onions
Pitted black olive slices
Guacamole
Salsa

Preheat oven to 350°F.

Place egg yolks, milk, flour and salt in blender or food processor container fitted with metal blade; process until smooth. Pour into bowl and let stand.

Melt butter in small skillet over medium heat. Add onion; cook until tender.

If using canned chiles, pat dry with paper towels. Slit each chili lengthwise and carefully remove seeds. Place 1 strip cheese and 1 tablespoon onion in each chili; reshape chiles to cover cheese. Place 2 chiles in each of 4 greased 1½-cup gratin dishes, or place in single layer in 13×9-inch baking dish.

Beat egg whites until soft peaks form; fold into yolk mixture. Dividing mixture evenly, pour over chiles in gratin dishes (or pour entire mixture over casserole).

Bake 20 to 25 minutes or until topping is puffed and knife inserted in center comes out clean. Broil 4 inches below heat 30 seconds or until topping is golden brown. Serve with condiments.   *Makes 4 servings*

Tidbit

Chiles rellenos literally means "stuffed peppers." The traditional Mexican version is made of fresh mild green chiles that have been stuffed with cheese, coated with egg batter and then fried until crisp.

Spinach Sensation

½ pound bacon slices
1 cup (8 ounces) sour cream
3 eggs, separated
2 tablespoons all-purpose flour
⅛ teaspoon black pepper
1 package (10 ounces) frozen chopped spinach, thawed and squeezed dry
½ cup (2 ounces) shredded sharp Cheddar cheese
½ cup dry bread crumbs
1 tablespoon margarine or butter, melted

Preheat oven to 350°F. Spray 2-quart round baking dish with nonstick cooking spray.

Place bacon in single layer in large skillet; cook over medium heat until crisp. Remove from skillet; drain on paper towels. Crumble and set aside.

Combine sour cream, egg yolks, flour and pepper in large bowl; set aside. Beat egg whites in medium bowl with electric mixer at high speed until stiff peaks form. Stir ¼ of egg whites into sour cream mixture; fold in remaining egg whites.

Arrange half of spinach in prepared dish. Top with half of sour cream mixture. Sprinkle ¼ cup cheese over sour cream mixture. Sprinkle bacon over cheese. Repeat layers, ending with remaining ¼ cup cheese.

Combine bread crumbs and margarine in small bowl; sprinkle evenly over cheese.

Bake, uncovered, 30 to 35 minutes or until egg mixture is set. Let stand 5 minutes before serving.

Makes 6 servings

Tidbit

Extra water from thawed spinach can affect the outcome of your dish. To remove excess moisture, put spinach between a double layer of paper towels and press until spinach is dry.

Spinach Sensation

Pizza for Breakfast

1 (6½-ounce) package pizza
  crust mix
1 pound BOB EVANS® Original
  Recipe Roll Sausage
1 cup diced fresh or drained
  canned tomatoes
8 ounces fresh mushrooms,
  sliced
1½ cups (6 ounces) shredded
  mozzarella cheese, divided
1½ cups (6 ounces) shredded
  sharp Cheddar cheese,
  divided
4 eggs
  Salt and pepper to taste
  Salsa (optional)

Preheat oven to 350°F. Prepare crust mix according to package directions. Spread pizza dough into greased 13×9-inch baking dish, making sure dough evenly covers bottom and 2 inches up sides of dish. Crumble and cook sausage in medium skillet until browned; drain well. Top crust with sausage, tomatoes, mushrooms, 1 cup mozzarella cheese and 1 cup Cheddar cheese. Bake 8 to 10 minutes or until crust is golden brown at edges. Remove from oven. Whisk eggs, salt and pepper in small bowl; pour over pizza. Return to oven; bake 7 to 9 minutes more or until eggs are set. Immediately sprinkle with remaining cheeses. Serve hot, with salsa, if desired. Refrigerate leftovers.

Makes 8 to 10 servings

Ham 'n Egg Special Strata

¼ cup butter
2 cups sliced fresh mushrooms
1 medium onion, finely
  chopped
2 cups diced cooked ham
8 slices white bread, cubed
4 eggs
2½ cups milk
2 cups (8 ounces) shredded
  cheddar cheese
1 tablespoon prepared mustard
1 teaspoon LAWRY'S®
  Seasoned Salt
  Dash LAWRY'S® Seasoned
  Pepper

In medium skillet, heat butter. Add mushrooms and onion and cook over medium-high heat until tender; stir in ham. In 13×9×2-inch baking dish, place bread cubes; arrange ham mixture over bread. In medium bowl, combine remaining ingredients; mix well. Pour over bread cubes, making sure all are moistened. Cover; refrigerate overnight. Bake, uncovered, in 325°F oven 55 to 60 minutes. Serve immediately.

Makes 6 to 8 servings

Pizza for Breakfast

Apple & Raisin Oven Pancake

1 large baking apple, cored
   and thinly sliced
⅓ cup golden raisins
2 tablespoons packed brown
   sugar
½ teaspoon ground cinnamon
4 eggs
⅔ cup milk
⅔ cup all-purpose flour
2 tablespoons butter or
   margarine, melted
   Powdered sugar (optional)

Preheat oven to 350°F. Spray
9-inch pie plate with nonstick
cooking spray.

Combine apple, raisins, brown
sugar and cinnamon in medium
bowl. Transfer to prepared pie
plate.

Bake, uncovered, 10 to 15 minutes
or until apple begins to soften.
Remove from oven. *Increase oven
temperature to 450°F.*

Meanwhile, whisk eggs, milk, flour
and butter in medium bowl until
blended. Pour batter over apple
mixture.

Bake 15 minutes or until pancake
is golden brown. Invert onto serving
dish. Sprinkle with powdered sugar,
if desired.   *Makes 6 servings*

Scalloped Eggs and Bacon

2 tablespoons butter or
   margarine
¼ cup chopped onion
2 tablespoons all-purpose flour
1½ cups milk
½ cup (2 ounces) shredded
   American cheese
½ cup (2 ounces) shredded
   Swiss cheese
6 hard-cooked eggs, sliced
10 to 12 slices HILLSHIRE
   FARM® Bacon, crisp-
   cooked and crumbled
1½ cups packaged fried onions

Preheat oven to 350°F.

Melt butter in medium skillet over
medium heat. Add chopped onion;
sauté until tender. Whisk in flour
until thoroughly combined. Add
milk; continue stirring until thick.
Add cheeses; stir until melted.
Place ½ of eggs in bottom of small
baking dish; pour ½ of cheese
mixture over eggs. Sprinkle with
½ of Bacon and ½ of fried onions.
Repeat layers. Bake, uncovered,
15 to 20 minutes or until heated
through.   *Makes 6 servings*

Apple & Raisin Oven Pancake

Make It Meaty

Pork Chops and Stuffing Bake

6 (¾-inch-thick) **boneless pork loin chops** (about 1½ **pounds**)
¼ **teaspoon salt**
⅛ **teaspoon black pepper**
1 tablespoon vegetable oil
1 small onion, chopped
2 ribs celery, chopped
2 Granny Smith apples, peeled, cored and coarsely chopped (about 2 cups)
1 can (14½ **ounces**) **reduced-sodium chicken broth**
1 can (10¾ **ounces**) **condensed cream of celery soup, undiluted**
¼ **cup dry white wine**
6 cups herb-seasoned stuffing cubes

pg. 22

pg. 30

Preheat oven to 375°F. Spray 13×9-inch baking dish with nonstick cooking spray.

Season both sides of pork chops with salt and pepper. Heat oil in large deep skillet over medium-high heat until hot. Add chops; cook until browned on both sides, turning once. Remove chops; set aside.

Add onion and celery to same skillet. Cook and stir 3 minutes or until onion is tender. Add apples; cook and stir 1 minute. Add broth, soup and wine; mix well. Bring to

continued on page 20

Pork Chop and Stuffing Bake

Pork Chops and Stuffing Bake,
continued

a simmer; remove from heat. Stir in stuffing cubes until evenly moistened.

Pour stuffing mixture into prepared dish, spreading evenly. Place pork chops on top of stuffing; pour any accumulated juices over chops.

Cover tightly with foil and bake 30 to 40 minutes or until pork chops are juicy and barely pink in center. *Makes 6 servings*

Easy Beef Lasagna

- **1 pound ground beef**
- **1 jar (26 to 28 ounces) RAGÚ® Old World Style® Pasta Sauce**
- **1 container (15 ounces) ricotta cheese**
- **2 cups shredded mozzarella cheese (about 8 ounces)**
- **½ cup grated Parmesan cheese, divided**
- **2 eggs**
- **12 lasagna noodles, cooked and drained**

1. Preheat oven to 375°F. In 12-inch skillet, brown ground beef; drain. Stir in Ragú Pasta Sauce; heat through.

2. In large bowl, combine ricotta cheese, mozzarella cheese, ¼ cup Parmesan cheese and eggs.

3. In 13×9-inch baking dish, evenly spread 1 cup meat sauce. Arrange 4 lasagna noodles lengthwise over sauce, then 1 cup meat sauce and ½ of the ricotta cheese mixture; repeat, ending with sauce. Cover with aluminum foil and bake 30 minutes. Sprinkle with remaining ¼ cup Parmesan cheese. Bake uncovered 5 minutes. Let stand 10 minutes before serving.
Makes 10 servings

Prep Time: 30 minutes
Cook Time: 35 minutes

Cheesy Ham Casserole

2 cups fresh or frozen broccoli flowerets, thawed
1½ cups KRAFT® Shredded Sharp Cheddar Cheese, divided
1½ cups coarsely chopped ham
1½ cups (4 ounces) corkscrew pasta, cooked, drained
½ cup MIRACLE WHIP® or MIRACLE WHIP® LIGHT® Dressing
½ green or red bell pepper, chopped
¼ cup milk
Seasoned croutons (optional)

● Heat oven to 350°F.

● Mix all ingredients except ½ cup cheese and croutons.

● Spoon into 1½-quart casserole. Sprinkle with remaining ½ cup cheese.

● Bake 30 minutes or until thoroughly heated. Sprinkle with croutons, if desired.

Makes 4 to 6 servings

Prep Time: 15 minutes
Cook Time: 30 minutes

Santa Fe Casserole Bake

1 pound ground beef
1 package (1.0 ounce) LAWRY'S® Taco Spices & Seasonings
2 cups chicken broth
¼ cup all-purpose flour
1 cup dairy sour cream
1 can (7 ounces) diced green chilies
1 package (11 ounces) corn or tortilla chips
2 cups (8 ounces) shredded Monterey Jack or cheddar cheese
½ cup sliced green onions with tops

In medium skillet, cook ground beef until browned and crumbly; drain fat. Add Taco Spices & Seasonings; mix well. In small saucepan, combine broth and flour; bring to a boil over medium-high heat to slightly thicken liquid. Stir in sour cream and chilies; mix well. In 13×9×2-inch lightly greased glass baking dish, place ½ of chips. Top with ½ of beef mixture, ½ of sauce, ½ of cheese and ½ of green onions. Layer again with remaining ingredients, ending with green onions. Bake, uncovered, in 375°F oven 20 minutes. Let stand 5 minutes before cutting.

Makes 6 servings

Tuscan Pot Pie

¾ **pound sweet or hot Italian sausage**
1 **jar (26 to 28 ounces) prepared chunky vegetable or mushroom spaghetti sauce**
1 **can (19 ounces) cannellini beans, rinsed and drained**
½ **teaspoon dried thyme leaves**
1½ **cups (6 ounces) shredded mozzarella cheese**
1 **package (8 ounces) refrigerated crescent dinner rolls**

1. Preheat oven to 425°F. Remove sausage from casings. Brown sausage in medium ovenproof skillet, stirring to separate meat. Drain drippings.

2. Add spaghetti sauce, beans and thyme to skillet. Simmer, uncovered, over medium heat 5 minutes. Remove from heat; stir in cheese.

3. Unroll crescent dough; divide into triangles. Arrange in spiral with points of dough towards center, covering sausage mixture completely. Bake 12 minutes or until crust is golden brown and meat mixture is bubbly.

Makes 4 to 6 servings

Prep and Cook Time: 27 minutes

Pork Chops and Yams

4 **pork chops (½ inch thick)**
2 **tablespoons oil**
2 **(16-ounce) cans yams or sweet potatoes, drained**
¾ **cup SMUCKER'S® Sweet Orange Marmalade or Apricot Preserves**
½ **large green bell pepper, cut into strips**
2 **tablespoons minced onion**

Brown pork chops in oil over medium heat.

Place yams in 1½-quart casserole. Stir in marmalade, bell pepper and onion. Layer pork chops over yam mixture. Cover and bake at 350°F for 30 minutes or until pork chops are tender.　*Makes 4 servings*

Tidbit

To remove a sausage casing, use a paring knife to slit the casing at one end. Be careful not to cut through the sausage. Grasp the cut edge and gently pull the casing away from the sausage.

Tuscan Pot Pie

Stuffed Bell Peppers

3 large bell peppers, any color, seeded and cut in half lengthwise
1½ cups chopped fresh tomatoes
1 tablespoon chopped fresh cilantro
1 jalapeño pepper,* seeded and chopped
1 clove garlic, finely minced
½ teaspoon dried oregano leaves, divided
¼ teaspoon ground cumin
8 ounces lean ground round
1 cup cooked brown rice
¼ cup cholesterol-free egg substitute *or* 2 egg whites
2 tablespoons finely chopped onion
¼ teaspoon salt
⅛ teaspoon black pepper

*Jalapeño peppers can sting and irritate the skin; wear rubber gloves when handling peppers and do not touch eyes. Wash hands after handling.

1. Preheat oven to 350°F.

2. Place steamer basket in large saucepan; add 1 inch of water, being careful not to let water touch bottom of basket. Place bell peppers in basket; cover. Bring to a boil; reduce heat to medium. Steam peppers 8 to 10 minutes or until tender, adding additional water if necessary; drain.

3. Combine tomatoes, cilantro, jalapeño pepper, garlic, ¼ teaspoon oregano and cumin in small bowl; set aside.

4. Thoroughly combine beef, rice, egg substitute, onion, salt and black pepper in large bowl. Stir 1 cup of tomato mixture into beef mixture. Spoon filling evenly into pepper halves; place in 13×9-inch baking dish. Cover tightly with foil.

5. Bake 45 minutes or until meat is browned and vegetables are tender. Serve with remaining tomato salsa, if desired.

Makes 6 servings

Tidbit

Keep skins of stuffed peppers supple by rubbing a little oil on the outsides of the peppers before baking.

Stuffed Bell Peppers

Pizza Pasta

- 1 tablespoon vegetable oil
- 1 medium green bell pepper, chopped
- 1 medium onion, chopped
- 1 cup sliced mushrooms
- ½ teaspoon LAWRY'S® Garlic Powder with Parsley OR Garlic Salt
- ¼ cup sliced ripe olives
- 1 package (1.5 ounces) LAWRY'S® Original-Style Spaghetti Sauce Spices & Seasonings
- 1¾ cups water
- 1 can (6 ounces) tomato paste
- 10 ounces mostaccioli, cooked and drained
- 3 ounces thinly sliced pepperoni
- ¾ cup shredded mozzarella cheese

In large skillet, heat vegetable oil; add bell pepper, onion, mushrooms and Garlic Powder with Parsley and cook over medium-high heat. Stir in olives, Spaghetti Sauce Spices & Seasonings, water and tomato paste; mix well. Bring sauce to a boil over medium-high heat; reduce heat to low and simmer, uncovered, 10 minutes. Add cooked mostaccioli and sliced pepperoni; mix well. Pour into 12×8×2-inch baking dish; top with cheese. Bake at 350°F 15 minutes until cheese is melted.

Makes 6 servings

Hunter's Pie

- 2 tablespoons salad oil
- 6 loin-cut lamb chops, cut into bite-size pieces
  LAWRY'S® Seasoned Salt to taste
  LAWRY'S® Seasoned Pepper to taste
- 4 cups mashed potatoes
- ¼ cup butter, melted
- ¼ teaspoon white pepper
- 1 side of 1 Twin Pack (1.95 ounces) LAWRY'S® Brown Gravy
- 1 cup water

In large skillet, heat oil and add lamb, Seasoned Salt and Seasoned Pepper; brown. Drain fat. In medium bowl, combine potatoes, butter and white pepper; blend well. Butter shallow casserole dish and line with half of potato mixture. Top with lamb. Spread remaining potatoes over top. Bake, uncovered, in 350°F oven 45 minutes. Meanwhile, in medium saucepan, prepare Brown Gravy with water according to package directions. Cut a hole in top of potato crust; pour about half of gravy into pie.

Makes 6 servings

Serving Suggestion: Pass remaining gravy at the table.

Hint: Use 1½ pounds cubed lamb or ground lamb, formed into meatballs, in place of loin chops.

Lamb & Pork Cassoulet

1 package (1 pound) dry white
    navy beans, rinsed
    Water
½ pound salt pork, sliced
1½ pounds boneless lamb
    shoulder or leg, cut into
    1-inch cubes
4 large pork chops
½ pound pork sausages
    Salt
    Pepper
2 large onions, chopped
1 can (28 ounces) tomatoes,
    drained
½ cup dry red wine
3 cloves garlic, finely chopped
¼ cup chopped fresh parsley
1 teaspoon dried thyme,
    crushed
1 bay leaf

Place beans in large bowl. Cover with cold water; soak overnight. Drain and rinse beans. Place beans in Dutch oven; cover with cold water. Bring to a boil over high heat, skimming foam as necessary. Reduce heat to low. Cover and simmer about 1 hour. Drain beans, reserving liquid.

Cook salt pork in large skillet over medium-high heat until some of the fat is rendered. Remove salt pork. In batches, brown lamb, pork chops and sausages in fat. Remove from skillet; drain on paper towels. Cut chops and sausages into 1-inch pieces.

Sprinkle meat with salt and pepper. Remove all but 2 tablespoons of the fat from skillet. Add onions. Cook and stir over medium-high heat until onions are tender. Add tomatoes, wine, garlic, parsley, thyme and bay leaf. Combine tomato mixture, drained beans and meats in large bowl. Spoon into large casserole. Pour reserved bean liquid over mixture just to cover. Bake at 350°F about 1½ hours or until meat is fork-tender. Remove bay leaf before serving.   *Makes 6 to 8 servings*

Favorite recipe from **American Lamb Council**

Southwestern-Style Beef Stew

¼ cup all-purpose flour
1 teaspoon seasoned salt
¼ teaspoon ground black pepper
2 pounds beef stew meat, cut into bite-size pieces
2 tablespoons vegetable oil
1 large onion, cut into wedges
2 large cloves garlic, finely chopped
1¾ cups (14½-ounce can) stewed tomatoes, undrained
1¾ cups (16-ounce jar) ORTEGA® Garden Style Salsa, mild
1 cup beef broth
1 tablespoon ground oregano
1 teaspoon ground cumin
½ teaspoon salt
3 large carrots, peeled, cut into 1-inch slices
1¾ cups (15-ounce can) garbanzo beans, drained
1 cup (8-ounce can) baby corn, drained, halved

COMBINE flour, salt and pepper in medium bowl or large resealable plastic food-storage bag. Add meat; toss well to coat.

HEAT oil in large saucepan over medium-high heat. Add meat, onion and garlic; cook for 5 to 6 minutes or until meat is browned on outside and onion is tender. Stir in tomatoes with juice, salsa, broth, oregano, cumin and salt. Bring to a boil; cover. Reduce heat to low; cook, stirring occasionally, for 45 minutes or until meat is tender.

STIR in carrots, beans and baby corn. Increase heat to medium-low. Cook, stirring occasionally, for 30 to 40 minutes or until carrots are tender.

Makes 8 servings

Tidbit

Garbanzo beans are also called chick-peas. These pale yellow legumes are somewhat round and have irregularly shaped surfaces. They are used in many Mediterranean, Middle Eastern and Indian dishes.

Southwestern-Style Beef Stew

Biscuit-Topped Hearty Steak Pie

1½ pounds top round steak, cooked and cut into 1-inch cubes
1 package (9 ounces) frozen baby carrots
1 package (9 ounces) frozen peas and pearl onions
1 large baking potato, cooked and cut into ½-inch pieces
1 jar (18 ounces) home-style brown gravy
½ teaspoon dried thyme leaves
½ teaspoon black pepper
1 can (10 ounces) refrigerated flaky buttermilk biscuits

Preheat oven to 375°F. Spray 2-quart casserole with nonstick cooking spray.

Combine steak, frozen vegetables and potato in prepared dish. Stir in gravy, thyme and pepper.

Bake, uncovered, 40 minutes. Remove from oven. *Increase oven temperature to 400°F.* Top with biscuits and bake 8 to 10 minutes or until biscuits are golden brown.
Makes 6 servings

Note: This casserole can be prepared with leftovers of almost any kind. Other steaks, roast beef, stew meat, pork, lamb or chicken can be substituted for round steak; adjust gravy flavor to complement meat.

Fix-It-Fast Corned Beef & Cabbage

1 small head cabbage (about 1½ pounds), cored and cut into 6 wedges
1 can (12 ounces) corned beef, sliced, *or* ½ pound sliced deli corned beef
1 can (14 ounces) sliced carrots, drained
1 can (16 ounces) sliced potatoes, drained
1⅓ cups *French's®* *Taste Toppers*™ French Fried Onions, divided
1 can (10¾ ounces) condensed cream of celery soup
¾ cup water

Preheat oven to 375°F. Arrange cabbage wedges and corned beef slices alternately down center of 13×9-inch baking dish. Place carrots, potatoes and ⅔ cup **Taste Toppers** along sides of dish. In small bowl, combine soup and water; pour over meat and vegetables. Bake, covered, at 375°F for 40 minutes or until cabbage is tender. Top with remaining ⅔ cup **Taste Toppers**; bake, uncovered, 3 minutes or until **Taste Toppers** are golden brown. *Makes 4 to 6 servings*

Biscuit-Topped Hearty Steak Pie

Potluck Poultry

pg. 36

pg. 46

Chicken Enchiladas

2 cups chopped cooked chicken
    or turkey
1 cup chopped green bell
    pepper
1 package (8 ounces)
    PHILADELPHIA® Cream
    Cheese, cubed
1 jar (8 ounces) salsa, divided
8 (6-inch) flour tortillas
¾ pound (12 ounces)
    VELVEETA® Pasteurized
    Process Cheese Spread,
    cut up
¼ cup milk

STIR chicken, bell pepper, cream cheese and ½ cup salsa in saucepan on low heat until cream cheese is melted.

SPOON ⅓ cup chicken mixture down center of each tortilla; roll up. Place, seam-side down, in lightly greased 12×8-inch baking dish.

STIR process cheese spread and milk in saucepan on low heat until smooth. Pour sauce over tortillas; cover with foil.

BAKE at 350°F for 20 minutes or until thoroughly heated. Pour remaining salsa over tortillas.
Makes 4 to 6 servings

Prep Time: 20 minutes
Bake Time: 20 minutes

Chicken Enchiladas

Spicy Turkey Casserole

1 tablespoon olive oil
1 pound turkey breast cutlets,
    cut into ½-inch pieces
2 (3-ounce) spicy chicken or
    turkey sausages, sliced
    ½ inch thick
1 cup diced green bell pepper
½ cup sliced mushrooms
½ cup diced onion
1 jalapeño pepper,* seeded
    and minced (optional)
½ cup fat-free reduced-sodium
    chicken broth or water
1 can (14 ounces) reduced-
    sodium diced tomatoes,
    undrained
1 teaspoon Italian seasoning
½ teaspoon paprika
¼ teaspoon black pepper
1 cup cooked egg yolk-free egg
    noodles
6 tablespoons grated Parmesan
    cheese
2 tablespoons coarse bread
    crumbs

*Jalapeño peppers can sting and irritate
the skin; wear rubber gloves when
handling peppers and do not touch
eyes. Wash hands after handling.

1. Preheat oven to 350°F. Heat oil
in large nonstick skillet. Add turkey
and sausages; cook and stir over
medium heat 2 minutes. Add bell
pepper, mushrooms, onion and
jalapeño pepper, if desired. Cook
and stir 5 minutes. Add chicken
broth; cook 1 minute, scraping
any browned bits off bottom of
skillet. Add tomatoes and liquid,
seasonings and noodles.

2. Spoon turkey mixture into
shallow 10-inch round casserole.
Sprinkle with cheese and bread
crumbs. Bake 15 to 20 minutes
or until mixture is hot and bread
crumbs are brown.

Makes 6 (1-cup) servings

Bayou Chicken Bake

4 to 6 PERDUE® Individually
    Frozen™ boneless, skinless
    chicken breasts
1½ to 2 teaspoons Cajun or
    Creole seasoning
½ cup chopped onion
1 cup uncooked regular
    long-grain rice
1 package (16 ounces) frozen
    black-eyed peas
2 cans (14½ ounces each)
    Cajun-style stewed
    tomatoes
2 tablespoons chopped fresh
    parsley

Preheat oven to 350°F. Lightly
grease 13×9-inch baking dish.
Sprinkle chicken with Cajun
seasoning; place in baking dish.
In large bowl, combine onion,
rice, black-eyed peas and tomatoes.
Pour over chicken. Cover and bake
45 minutes. Uncover and bake
15 minutes longer, or until chicken
is cooked through. Sprinkle with
parsley before serving.

Makes 4 to 6 servings

Spicy Turkey Casserole

Chicken Marsala

4 cups (6 ounces) uncooked
    broad egg noodles
½ cup Italian-style dry bread
    crumbs
1 teaspoon dried basil leaves
1 egg
1 teaspoon water
4 boneless skinless chicken
    breast halves
3 tablespoons olive oil, divided
¾ cup chopped onion
8 ounces cremini or button
    mushrooms, sliced
3 cloves garlic, minced
3 tablespoons all-purpose flour
1 can (14½ ounces) chicken
    broth
½ cup dry marsala wine
¾ teaspoon salt
¼ teaspoon black pepper
    Chopped fresh parsley
    (optional)

Preheat oven to 375°F. Spray
11×7-inch baking dish with
nonstick cooking spray.

Cook noodles according to
package directions until al dente.
Drain and place in prepared dish.

Meanwhile, combine bread
crumbs and basil on shallow plate
or pie plate. Beat egg with water
on another shallow plate or pie
plate. Dip chicken in egg mixture,
letting excess drip off. Roll in
crumb mixture, patting to coat.

Heat 2 tablespoons oil in large
skillet over medium-high heat until
hot. Cook chicken 3 minutes per
side or until browned. Transfer to
clean plate; set aside.

Heat remaining 1 tablespoon oil in
same skillet over medium heat.
Add onion; cook and stir 5 minutes.
Add mushrooms and garlic; cook
and stir 3 minutes. Sprinkle onion
mixture with flour; cook and stir
1 minute. Add broth, wine, salt
and pepper; bring to a boil over
high heat. Cook and stir 5 minutes
or until sauce thickens.

Reserve ½ cup sauce. Pour
remaining sauce over cooked
noodles; stir until noodles are well
coated. Place chicken on top of
noodles. Spoon reserved sauce
over chicken.

Bake, uncovered, about 20 minutes
or until chicken is no longer pink
in center and sauce is hot and
bubbly. Sprinkle with parsley, if
desired. *Makes 4 servings*

Chicken Marsala

Chicken & Biscuits

¼ cup butter or margarine
4 boneless skinless chicken
   breast halves (about
   1¼ pounds), cut into
   ½-inch pieces
½ cup chopped onion
½ teaspoon dried thyme leaves
½ teaspoon paprika
¼ teaspoon black pepper
1 can (about 14 ounces)
   chicken broth, divided
⅓ cup all-purpose flour
1 package (10 ounces) frozen
   peas and carrots
1 can (12 ounces) refrigerated
   biscuits

Preheat oven to 375°F. Melt butter in large skillet over medium heat. Add chicken, onion, thyme, paprika and pepper. Cook 5 minutes or until chicken is browned.

Combine ¼ cup chicken broth with flour; stir until smooth. Set aside.

Add remaining chicken broth to skillet; bring to a boil. Gradually add flour mixture, stirring constantly to prevent lumps from forming. Simmer 5 minutes. Add peas and carrots; continue cooking 2 minutes.

Transfer to 1½-quart casserole; top with biscuits. Bake 25 to 30 minutes or until biscuits are golden brown.

Makes 4 to 6 servings

Fettuccine with Chicken Breasts

12 ounces uncooked fettuccine
   or egg noodles
1 cup HIDDEN VALLEY®
   Original Ranch® Dressing
⅓ cup Dijon mustard
8 boneless, skinless chicken
   breast halves, pounded
   thin
½ cup butter
⅓ cup dry white wine

Cook fettuccine according to package directions; drain. Preheat oven to 425°F. Stir together dressing and mustard; set aside. Pour fettuccine into oiled baking dish. Sauté chicken in butter in a large skillet until no longer pink in center. Transfer cooked chicken to the bed of fettuccine. Add wine to the skillet; cook until reduced to desired consistency. Drizzle over chicken. Pour the reserved dressing mixture over the chicken. Bake at 425°F about 10 minutes, or until dressing forms a golden brown crust.   *Makes 8 servings*

Chicken & Biscuits

Creamy Chicken and Pasta with Spinach

6 ounces uncooked egg noodles
1 tablespoon olive oil
¼ cup chopped onion
¼ cup chopped red bell pepper
1 package (10 ounces) frozen spinach, thawed and drained
2 boneless skinless chicken breast halves (¾ pound), cooked and cut into 1-inch pieces
1 can (4 ounces) sliced mushrooms, drained
2 cups (8 ounces) shredded Swiss cheese
1 container (8 ounces) sour cream
¾ cup half-and-half
2 eggs, slightly beaten
½ teaspoon salt
  Red onion and fresh spinach for garnish

Preheat oven to 350°F. Prepare egg noodles according to package directions; set aside.

Heat oil in large skillet over medium-high heat. Add onion and bell pepper; cook and stir 2 minutes or until onion is tender. Add spinach, chicken, mushrooms and cooked noodles; stir to combine.

Combine cheese, sour cream, half-and-half, eggs and salt in medium bowl; blend well.

Add cheese mixture to chicken mixture; stir to combine. Pour into 13×9-inch baking dish coated with nonstick cooking spray. Bake, covered, 30 to 35 minutes or until heated through. Garnish with red onion and fresh spinach, if desired.
Makes 8 servings

Brown Rice Chicken Bake

3 cups cooked brown rice
1 package (10 ounces) frozen green peas
2 cups chopped cooked chicken breasts
½ cup cholesterol free, reduced calorie mayonnaise
⅓ cup slivered almonds, toasted (optional)
2 teaspoons soy sauce
¼ teaspoon ground black pepper
¼ teaspoon garlic powder
¼ teaspoon dried tarragon leaves
  Vegetable cooking spray

Spray 3-quart baking casserole with cooking spray. Combine rice, peas, chicken, mayonnaise, almonds, soy sauce, and seasonings in large bowl; mix well. Spoon into prepared casserole; cover. Bake at 350°F for 15 to 20 minutes or until heated through.   *Makes 6 servings*

Favorite recipe from **USA Rice Federation**

Turkey Manicotti

1 pound Italian turkey sausage
¼ pound fresh mushrooms, chopped
½ cup onion, chopped
1 clove garlic, minced
1½ cups low-fat ricotta cheese
1 cup (4 ounces) part-skim mozzarella cheese, grated
1 egg, beaten
1 package (10 ounces) frozen chopped spinach, defrosted and well drained
1 package (8 ounces) manicotti shells, cooked according to package directions and drained
Vegetable cooking spray
¼ cup flour
⅛ teaspoon pepper
1 can (15 ounces) evaporated skim milk
½ cup low-sodium chicken broth
½ cup plus 2 tablespoons Parmesan cheese

1. In large non-stick skillet, over medium heat, sauté turkey sausage, mushrooms, onion and garlic 5 to 6 minutes or until sausage is no longer pink. Remove skillet from heat and drain.

2. In large bowl combine ricotta cheese, mozzarella cheese and egg. Combine with turkey sausage mixture and spinach.

3. Cut each manicotti shell open down long side. This will make stuffing shells easier. Carefully spoon ⅓ cup turkey sausage filling down center of each shell. Roll up shell to encase turkey filling. Arrange stuffed shells, seam-side-down, on (11×14-inch) baking dish lightly coated with vegetable spray.

4. In medium saucepan combine flour and pepper. With wire whisk slowly combine evaporated milk and chicken broth with flour and pepper. Over medium heat, stirring constantly, heat sauce until it begins to boil and thickens. Remove pan from heat; whisk in ½ cup Parmesan cheese. Pour sauce over stuffed shells; sprinkle with remaining Parmesan cheese.

5. Cover baking pan with foil. Bake in 350° F. oven 20 to 25 minutes or until mixture is heated through.
Makes 8 servings

Favorite recipe from **National Turkey Federation**

Spinach Quiche

1 medium leek
¼ cup butter or margarine
2 cups finely chopped cooked chicken
½ package (10 ounces) frozen chopped spinach or broccoli, cooked and drained
1 unbaked ready-to-use pie crust (10 inches in diameter)
1 tablespoon all-purpose flour
1½ cups (6 ounces) shredded Swiss cheese
1½ cups half-and-half or evaporated milk
4 eggs
2 tablespoons brandy
½ teaspoon salt
¼ teaspoon black pepper
¼ teaspoon ground nutmeg

Preheat oven to 375°F. Cut leek in half lengthwise; wash and trim, leaving 2 to 3 inches of green tops intact. Cut leek halves crosswise into thin slices. Place in small saucepan; add enough water to cover. Bring to a boil over high heat; reduce heat and simmer 5 minutes. Drain; reserve leek.

Melt butter in large skillet over medium heat. Add chicken; cook until chicken is golden, about 5 minutes. Add spinach and leek to chicken mixture; cook 1 to 2 minutes longer. Remove from heat.

Spoon chicken mixture into pie crust. Sprinkle flour and cheese over chicken mixture. Combine half-and-half, eggs, brandy, salt, pepper and nutmeg in medium bowl. Pour egg mixture over cheese.

Bake 35 to 40 minutes or until knife inserted into center comes out clean. Let stand 5 minutes before serving. Serve hot or cold.

Makes 6 servings

Tidbit

A leek looks like an oversized scallion. It consists of long, flat, dark green leaves on top, and a white tubular base. Its root end is bulbous–similar to that of a scallion.

Spinach Quiche

Broccoli Cheese Casserole

3 whole chicken breasts,
  skinned and halved
1½ pounds fresh broccoli
2 tablespoons margarine
½ cup chopped onion
1 clove garlic, minced
3 tablespoons all-purpose flour
1¼ cups skim milk
2 tablespoons fresh parsley
½ teaspoon salt
½ teaspoon dried oregano
  leaves, crushed
1½ cups 1% low fat cream-style
  small curd cottage cheese
1½ cups shredded reduced fat
  Wisconsin Cheddar cheese
¼ cup grated Wisconsin
  Romano cheese
1 jar (4½ ounces) sliced
  mushrooms, drained
6 ounces noodles, cooked and
  drained

MICROWAVE DIRECTIONS
Place chicken breasts in microwavable glass baking dish. Microwave at HIGH (100% power) 7 minutes. Cool slightly and cube. Set aside. Remove flowerets from broccoli and cut larger ones in half. Cut stems into 1-inch pieces. Place broccoli in 3-quart microwavable baking dish with ½ cup water. Cover and microwave at HIGH (100% power) 7 minutes, stirring once. Let stand, covered, 2 minutes. Drain well; set aside.

Place margarine, onion and garlic in same baking dish. Cover and microwave at HIGH (100% power) 3 minutes. Stir in flour. Gradually add milk. Add parsley, salt and oregano. Microwave at HIGH (100% power) 1 minute. Stir well; microwave 1 minute. Stir in cottage cheese. Microwave at HIGH (100% power) 2 minutes. Stir; microwave 2 minutes. Add Cheddar and Romano cheeses, stirring well. Microwave at MEDIUM-HIGH (70% power) 2 minutes. Stir in chicken, broccoli, mushrooms and noodles. Cover and microwave at MEDIUM (50% power) 5 minutes or until heated through.

Makes 6 to 8 servings

Favorite recipe from ***Wisconsin Milk Marketing Board***

Trim Turkey Tetrazzini

½ pound BUTTERBALL® Oven Roasted Turkey Breast, sliced ½ inch thick in the deli, cubed
½ pound uncooked spaghetti, broken
¼ cup butter or margarine
¼ cup flour
1 can (14½ ounces) fat free reduced sodium chicken broth
2¾ cups milk
½ teaspoon salt
¼ teaspoon ground white pepper
8 ounces fresh mushrooms, sliced
¼ cup grated Parmesan cheese
½ cup crumbled salad croutons

Cook and drain spaghetti. Melt butter in large skillet over medium heat. Whisk in flour. Add chicken broth, milk, salt and pepper. Heat, stirring constantly, until thickened. Add turkey, mushrooms, Parmesan cheese and spaghetti to skillet. Spray 13×9-inch baking dish with nonstick cooking spray. Pour turkey mixture into baking dish. Top with crumbled croutons. Bake 30 to 40 minutes in preheated 350°F oven. *Makes 8 servings*

Preparation Time: 15 minutes plus baking time

Chilaquiles

1 can (10¾ ounces) condensed cream of chicken soup
½ cup mild green chili salsa
1 can (4 ounces) diced green chilies, undrained
8 cups taco chips
2 to 3 cups shredded cooked turkey or chicken
2 cups (8 ounces) shredded Cheddar cheese
Sliced pitted black olives for garnish
Cilantro sprigs for garnish

Preheat oven to 350°F. Combine soup and salsa in medium bowl; stir in green chilies. Place ⅓ of chips in 2- to 2½-quart casserole; top with ⅓ of turkey. Spread ⅓ of soup mixture over turkey; sprinkle with ⅓ of cheese. Repeat layering. Bake, uncovered, 15 minutes or until casserole is heated through and cheese is melted. Garnish with olives and cilantro.
Makes 6 servings

Turkey Vegetable Crescent Pie

2 cans (about 14 ounces) fat-free reduced-sodium chicken broth
1 medium onion, diced
1¼ pounds turkey tenderloins, cut into ¾-inch pieces
3 cups diced red potatoes
1 teaspoon chopped fresh rosemary *or* ½ teaspoon dried rosemary
¼ teaspoon salt
⅛ teaspoon black pepper
1 bag (16 ounces) frozen mixed vegetables
1 bag (10 ounces) frozen mixed vegetables
⅓ cup fat-free (skim) milk plus additional if necessary
3 tablespoons cornstarch
1 package (8 ounces) refrigerated reduced-fat crescent rolls

1. Bring broth to a boil in large saucepan. Add onion; reduce heat and simmer 3 minutes. Add turkey; return to a boil. Reduce heat; cover and simmer 7 to 9 minutes or until turkey is no longer pink. Remove turkey from saucepan with slotted spoon; place in 13×9-inch baking dish.

2. Return broth to a boil. Add potatoes, rosemary, salt and pepper; simmer 2 minutes. Return to a boil; stir in mixed vegetables. Simmer, covered, 7 to 8 minutes or until potatoes are tender.

Remove vegetables with slotted spoon. Drain in colander set over bowl; reserve broth. Transfer vegetables to baking dish with turkey.

3. Preheat oven to 375°F. Blend ⅓ cup milk with cornstarch in small bowl until smooth. Add enough milk to reserved broth to equal 3 cups. Heat in large saucepan over medium-high heat; whisk in cornstarch mixture, stirring constantly until mixture comes to a boil. Boil 1 minute; remove from heat. Pour over turkey-vegetable mixture in baking dish.

4. Roll out crescent roll dough; separate at perforations. Arrange dough pieces decoratively over top of turkey-vegetable mixture. Bake 13 to 15 minutes or until crust is golden brown.

Makes 8 servings

Turkey Vegetable Crescent Pie

Deep-Sea Dishes

Shrimp Primavera Pot Pie

1 can (10¾ ounces) condensed cream of shrimp soup, undiluted
1 package (12 ounces) frozen peeled uncooked medium shrimp
2 packages (1 pound each) frozen mixed vegetables, such as green beans, potatoes, onions and red peppers, thawed and drained
1 teaspoon dried dill weed
¼ teaspoon salt
¼ teaspoon black pepper
1 package (11 ounces) refrigerated soft breadstick dough

1. Preheat oven to 400°F. Heat soup in medium ovenproof skillet over medium-high heat 1 minute. Add shrimp; cook and stir 3 minutes or until shrimp begin to thaw. Stir in vegetables, dill, salt and pepper; mix well. Reduce heat to medium-low; cook and stir 3 minutes.

2. Unwrap breadstick dough; separate into 8 strips. Twist strips, cutting to fit skillet. Arrange attractively over shrimp mixture. Press ends of dough lightly to edges of skillet to secure. Bake 18 minutes or until crust is golden brown and shrimp mixture is bubbly.

Makes 4 to 6 servings

pg. 52

pg. 60

Shrimp Primavera Pot Pie

Jambalaya

1 teaspoon vegetable oil
½ pound smoked deli ham, cubed
½ pound smoked sausage, cut into ¼-inch-thick slices
1 large onion, chopped
1 large green bell pepper, chopped (about 1½ cups)
3 ribs celery, chopped (about 1 cup)
3 cloves garlic, minced
1 can (28 ounces) diced tomatoes, undrained
1 can (10½ ounces) chicken broth
1 cup uncooked rice
1 tablespoon Worcestershire sauce
1 teaspoon salt
1 teaspoon dried thyme leaves
½ teaspoon black pepper
¼ teaspoon ground red pepper
1 package (12 ounces) frozen ready-to-cook shrimp, thawed
Fresh chives (optional)

Preheat oven to 350°F. Spray 13×9-inch baking dish with nonstick cooking spray.

Heat oil in large skillet over medium-high heat until hot. Add ham and sausage. Cook and stir 5 minutes or until sausage is lightly browned on both sides. Remove from skillet and place in prepared dish. Place onion, bell pepper, celery and garlic in same skillet; cook and stir 3 minutes. Add to sausage mixture.

Combine tomatoes with juice, broth, rice, Worcestershire, salt, thyme, black pepper and red pepper in same skillet; bring to a boil over high heat. Reduce heat to low and simmer 3 minutes. Pour over sausage mixture and stir until combined.

Cover tightly with foil and bake 45 minutes or until rice is almost tender. Remove from oven; place shrimp on top of rice mixture. Bake, uncovered, 10 minutes or until shrimp are pink and opaque. Garnish with chives, if desired.

Makes 8 servings

Tidbit

The French word for ham, "jambon," is believed to be the basis for this dish's name–"jambalaya." Ham was a main ingredient in many traditional versions of this recipe. Today, jambalaya is symbolic of creole cooking.

Jambalaya

Tuna Pot Pie

1 tablespoon margarine or
    butter
1 small onion, chopped
1 can (10¾ ounces) condensed
    cream of potato soup,
    undiluted
¼ cup milk
½ teaspoon dried thyme leaves
¼ teaspoon salt
⅛ teaspoon black pepper
2 cans (6 ounces each) albacore
    tuna in water, drained
1 package (16 ounces) frozen
    vegetable medley (such as
    broccoli, green beans,
    carrots and red peppers),
    thawed
2 tablespoons chopped fresh
    parsley
1 can (8 ounces) refrigerated
    crescent roll dough

Preheat oven to 350°F. Spray
11×7-inch baking dish with
nonstick cooking spray.

Melt margarine in large skillet over
medium heat. Add onion; cook
and stir 2 minutes or until onion is
tender. Add soup, milk, thyme, salt
and pepper; cook and stir 3 to
4 minutes or until thick and
bubbly. Stir in tuna, vegetables
and parsley. Pour mixture into
prepared dish.

Unroll crescent roll dough and
divide into triangles. Place
triangles over tuna filling without
overlapping dough.

Bake, uncovered, 20 minutes or
until triangles are golden brown.
Let stand 5 minutes before serving.
Garnish as desired.

Makes 6 servings

Fillets Stuffed with Crabmeat

1 envelope LIPTON® RECIPE
    SECRETS® Savory Herb
    with Garlic Soup Mix*
½ cup fresh bread crumbs
1 package (6 ounces) frozen
    crabmeat, thawed and
    well-drained
½ cup water
2 teaspoons lemon juice
4 fish fillets (about 1 pound)
1 tablespoon margarine or
    butter, melted

*Also terrific with LIPTON® RECIPE
SECRETS® Golden Onion Soup Mix.

Preheat oven to 350°F.

In medium bowl, combine soup
mix, bread crumbs, crabmeat,
water and lemon juice.

Top fillets evenly with crabmeat
mixture; roll up and secure with
wooden toothpicks. Place in lightly
greased 2-quart oblong baking dish.
Brush fish with margarine and bake
25 minutes or until fish flakes.
Remove toothpicks before serving.

Makes 4 servings

Tuna Pot Pie

Jumbo Shells Seafood Fancies

1 package (16 ounces)
   uncooked jumbo pasta
   shells
1 can (7½ ounces) crabmeat
4 ounces (1 cup) grated Swiss
   cheese
1 can (2½ ounces) tiny shrimp,
   drained
½ cup mayonnaise
2 tablespoons thinly sliced
   celery
1 tablespoon chopped onion
1 tablespoon finely chopped
   pimiento

1. Cook shells according to package directions until tender but still firm; drain. Rinse under cold running water; drain again.

2. Invert shells onto paper towel-lined plate to drain and cool.

3. Drain and discard liquid from crabmeat. Place crabmeat in large bowl; flake with fork into small pieces. Remove any bits of shell or cartilage.

4. Add remaining ingredients to crabmeat. If mixture seems too dry, add more mayonnaise.

5. Using large spoon, stuff cooled shells with seafood mixture.

6. Cover; refrigerate until chilled. Garnish, if desired.

Makes 8 servings

Sole Almondine

1 package (6.5 ounces)
   RICE-A-RONI® Broccoli
   Au Gratin
1 medium zucchini
4 sole, scrod or orange roughy
   fillets
1 tablespoon lemon juice
¼ cup grated Parmesan cheese,
   divided
   Salt and pepper (optional)
¼ cup sliced almonds
2 tablespoons margarine or
   butter, melted

1. Prepare Rice-A-Roni® Mix as package directs.

2. While Rice-A-Roni® is simmering, cut zucchini lengthwise into 12 thin strips. Heat oven to 350°F.

3. In 11×7-inch glass baking dish, spread prepared rice evenly. Set aside. Sprinkle fish with lemon juice, 2 tablespoons cheese, salt and pepper, if desired. Place zucchini strips over fish; roll up. Place fish seam-side down on rice.

4. Combine almonds and margarine; sprinkle evenly over fish. Top with remaining 2 tablespoons cheese. Bake 20 to 25 minutes or until fish flakes easily with fork.

Makes 4 servings

Tuna-Noodle Casserole

1 tablespoon butter
¾ cup diced onion
1 can cream of mushroom soup
1 cup milk
3 cups hot cooked egg noodles
2 cans tuna, drained and flaked
1¼ cups frozen peas
1 jar diced pimientos, drained
1 tablespoon lemon juice
¼ teaspoon salt
¼ teaspoon black pepper
½ cup fresh bread crumbs
½ cup grated BELGIOIOSO® Parmesan Cheese

Preheat oven to 450°F. Melt butter in medium saucepan over medium-high heat. Add onion; sauté 3 minutes. Add soup and milk. Cook 3 minutes, whisking constantly. Combine soup mixture, noodles, tuna, peas, pimientos, lemon juice, salt and pepper in 2-quart casserole. Combine bread crumbs and BelGioioso Parmesan Cheese in separate bowl; sprinkle on top of tuna mixture. Bake at 450°F for 15 minutes or until bubbly. *Makes 4 servings*

Shrimp Casserole

¾ pound raw medium Florida shrimp, peeled, deveined
⅓ cup chopped celery
¼ cup chopped onion
¼ cup chopped green bell pepper
3 tablespoons margarine
1 can (10¾ ounces) condensed cream of celery soup
½ cup dry stuffing mix
1 hard-boiled egg, chopped
⅓ cup sliced water chestnuts
1 tablespoon lemon juice
¼ teaspoon salt
¼ cup (1 ounce) shredded Cheddar cheese

MICROWAVE DIRECTIONS
Halve large shrimp. In 1½-quart shallow casserole, combine shrimp, celery, onion, bell pepper and margarine. Cover; cook on HIGH 4 minutes, stirring after 2 minutes. Stir in soup, stuffing mix, egg, water chestnuts, juice and salt. Cover; cook on HIGH 4 minutes. Sprinkle with cheese; cook, uncovered, on HIGH 1 minute. *Makes 4 servings*

Favorite recipe from **Florida Department of Agriculture and Consumer Services, Bureau of Seafood and Aquaculture**

Pasta with Salmon and Dill

6 ounces uncooked mafalda pasta
1 tablespoon olive oil
2 ribs celery, sliced
1 small red onion, chopped
1 can (10¾ ounces) condensed cream of celery soup
¼ cup reduced-fat mayonnaise
¼ cup dry white wine
3 tablespoons chopped fresh parsley
1 teaspoon dried dill weed
1 can (7½ ounces) pink salmon, drained
½ cup dry bread crumbs
1 tablespoon margarine or butter, melted
  Fresh dill sprigs (optional)
  Red onion slices (optional)

Preheat oven to 350°F. Spray 1-quart square baking dish with nonstick cooking spray.

Cook pasta according to package directions until al dente; drain and set aside.

Meanwhile, heat oil in medium skillet over medium-high heat until hot. Add celery and onion; cook and stir 2 minutes or until vegetables are tender. Set aside.

Combine soup, mayonnaise, wine, parsley and dill weed in large bowl. Stir in pasta, vegetables and salmon until pasta is well coated. Pour salmon mixture into prepared dish.

Combine bread crumbs and margarine in small bowl; sprinkle evenly over casserole. Bake, uncovered, 25 minutes or until hot and bubbly. Garnish with dill sprigs and onion slices, if desired.
Makes 4 servings

Seafood Quiche

1 package (8 ounces) PHILADELPHIA® Cream Cheese, softened
1 can (6 ounces) crabmeat, drained, flaked
4 eggs
½ cup sliced green onions
½ cup milk
½ teaspoon dill weed
½ teaspoon lemon and pepper seasoning salt
1 (9-inch) baked pastry shell

MIX all ingredients except pastry shell with electric mixer on medium speed until well blended.

POUR into pastry shell.

BAKE at 350°F for 40 minutes or until knife inserted in center comes out clean. Let stand 10 minutes before serving.
Makes 6 to 8 servings

Prep Time: 15 minutes
Bake Time: 40 minutes plus standing

Pasta with Salmon and Dill

Shrimp Noodle Supreme

1 package (8 ounces) spinach noodles, cooked and drained
1 package (3 ounces) cream cheese, cubed and softened
1½ pounds medium shrimp, peeled and deveined
½ cup butter, softened
Salt
Black pepper
1 can (10¾ ounces) condensed cream of mushroom soup
1 cup sour cream
½ cup half-and-half
½ cup mayonnaise
1 tablespoon snipped chives
1 tablespoon chopped fresh parsley
½ teaspoon Dijon mustard
¾ cup (6 ounces) shredded sharp Cheddar cheese

Preheat oven to 325°F. Combine noodles and cream cheese in medium bowl. Spread noodle mixture into bottom of greased 13×9-inch glass casserole. Cook shrimp in butter in large skillet over medium-high heat until pink and tender, about 5 minutes. Season to taste with salt and pepper. Spread shrimp over noodles.

Combine soup, sour cream, half-and-half, mayonnaise, chives, parsley and mustard in another medium bowl. Spread over shrimp.

Sprinkle Cheddar cheese over top. Bake 25 minutes or until hot and cheese is melted. Garnish, if desired. *Makes 6 servings*

Fish a la Paolo

1 (16-ounce) jar NEWMAN'S OWN® Medium Salsa
1 (10-ounce) package frozen chopped spinach, thawed, drained and squeezed dry (or favorite mild vegetable)
2 tablespoons capers
1 tablespoon lemon juice
1 pound firm fresh fish, such as scrod fillets, cut into 4 pieces
1 tablespoon butter, cut into small pieces
1 large tomato, thinly sliced
½ cup fresh cilantro leaves, chopped

Preheat oven to 400°F. Mix salsa with spinach, capers and lemon juice; place in bottom of 11×7-inch baking dish. Place fish on top. Dot fish with butter and top with tomato slices.

Bake 25 minutes. Remove from oven and top with chopped cilantro. *Makes 4 servings*

Shrimp Noodle Supreme

Paella

¼ cup **FILIPPO BERIO® Olive Oil**
1 **pound boneless skinless chicken breasts, cut into 1-inch strips**
½ **pound Italian sausage, cut into 1-inch slices**
1 **onion, chopped**
3 **cloves garlic, minced**
2 **(14½-ounce) cans chicken broth**
2 **cups uncooked long grain white rice**
1 **(8-ounce) bottle clam juice**
1 **(2-ounce) jar chopped pimientos, drained**
2 **bay leaves**
1 **teaspoon salt**
¼ **teaspoon saffron threads, crumbled (optional)**
1 **pound raw shrimp, shelled and deveined**
1 **(16-ounce) can whole tomatoes, drained**
1 **(10-ounce) package frozen peas, thawed**
12 **littleneck clams, scrubbed**
¼ **cup water**
   Fresh herb sprig (optional)

Preheat oven to 350°F. In large skillet, heat olive oil over medium heat until hot. Add chicken; cook and stir 8 to 10 minutes or until brown on all sides. Remove with slotted spoon; set aside. Add sausage to skillet; cook and stir 8 to 10 minutes or until brown. Remove with slotted spoon; set aside. Add onion and garlic to skillet; cook and stir 5 to 7 minutes or until onion is tender. Transfer chicken, sausage, onion and garlic mixture to large casserole.

Add chicken broth, rice, clam juice, pimiento, bay leaves, salt and saffron, if desired, to chicken mixture. Cover; bake 30 minutes. Add shrimp, tomatoes and peas; stir well. Cover; bake an additional 15 minutes or until rice is tender, liquid is absorbed and shrimp are opaque. Remove bay leaves.

Meanwhile, combine clams and water in stockpot or large saucepan. Cover; cook over medium heat 5 to 10 minutes or until clams open; remove clams immediately as they open. Discard any clams with unopened shells. Place clams on top of paella. Garnish with herb sprig, if desired.

Makes 4 to 6 servings

Tidbit

Make sure only to buy clams with tightly closed shells. If any of them are even slightly open, tap them lightly. Live clams will snap shut. Discard any that don't snap shut.

Paella

Meatless Meals

Three Cheese Baked Ziti

1 container (15 ounces) part-skim ricotta cheese
2 eggs, beaten
¼ cup grated Parmesan cheese
1 box (16 ounces) ziti pasta, cooked and drained
1 jar (28 ounces) RAGÚ® Chunky Gardenstyle Pasta Sauce
1 cup shredded mozzarella cheese (about 4 ounces)

Preheat oven to 350°F. In large bowl, combine ricotta cheese, eggs and Parmesan cheese; set aside.

In another bowl, thoroughly combine pasta and Ragú® Chunky Gardenstyle Pasta Sauce.

In 13×9-inch baking dish, spoon ½ of the pasta mixture; evenly top with ricotta cheese mixture, then remaining pasta mixture. Sprinkle with mozzarella cheese. Bake 30 minutes or until heated through. Serve, if desired, with additional heated pasta sauce.

Makes 8 servings

pg. 68

pg. 74

Three Cheese Baked Ziti

Cannelloni with Tomato-Eggplant Sauce

Tomato-Eggplant Sauce
(recipe follows)
1 package (10 ounces) fresh
   spinach
1 cup fat-free ricotta cheese
4 egg whites, beaten
¼ cup (1 ounce) grated
   Parmesan cheese
2 tablespoons finely chopped
   fresh parsley
½ teaspoon salt (optional)
8 manicotti (about 4 ounces),
   cooked and cooled
1 cup (4 ounces) shredded
   reduced-fat mozzarella
   cheese

1. Preheat oven to 350°F. Prepare Tomato-Eggplant Sauce.

2. Wash spinach; do not pat dry. Place spinach in saucepan; cook, covered, over medium-high heat 3 to 5 minutes or until spinach is wilted. Cool slightly and drain; chop finely.

3. Combine ricotta cheese, spinach, egg whites, Parmesan cheese, parsley and salt, if desired, in large bowl; mix well. Spoon mixture into manicotti shells; arrange in 13×9-inch baking pan. Spoon Tomato-Eggplant Sauce over manicotti; sprinkle with mozzarella cheese.

4. Bake manicotti, uncovered, 25 to 30 minutes or until hot and bubbly. Garnish as desired.

*Makes 4 servings
(2 manicotti each)*

Tomato-Eggplant Sauce

Olive oil-flavored nonstick
   cooking spray
1 small eggplant, coarsely
   chopped
½ cup chopped onion
2 cloves garlic, minced
½ teaspoon dried tarragon
   leaves
¼ teaspoon dried thyme leaves
1 can (16 ounces) no-salt-
   added whole tomatoes,
   undrained and coarsely
   chopped
Salt
Black pepper

1. Spray large skillet with cooking spray; heat over medium heat until hot. Add eggplant, onion, garlic, tarragon and thyme; cook and stir about 5 minutes or until vegetables are tender.

2. Stir in tomatoes with juice; bring to a boil. Reduce heat and simmer, uncovered, 3 to 4 minutes. Season to taste with salt and pepper.

Makes about 2½ cups

Cannelloni with Tomato-Eggplant Sauce

Mediterranean Strata

2 pounds green zucchini or
   yellow squash, cut into
   ¼-inch slices
1 cup ricotta cheese
3 eggs
1½ cups milk, heavy cream or
   half 'n' half cream
1 cup minced fresh basil
   (2 bunches)
2 tablespoons all-purpose flour
1 tablespoon minced garlic
1 cup shredded mozzarella
   cheese
1 cup *French's® Taste Toppers™*
   French Fried Onions

1. Preheat oven to 350°F. Place
zucchini and *2 tablespoons water*
into 2-quart microwave-safe baking
dish. Cover with vented plastic
wrap. Microwave on HIGH
3 minutes or until just tender;
drain well.

2. Whisk together ricotta cheese,
eggs, milk, basil, flour, garlic and
½ teaspoon salt in large bowl. Pour
over zucchini. Sprinkle with cheese.
Bake, uncovered, 50 minutes or
until custard is just set.

3. Sprinkle with mozzarella
cheese and ***Taste Toppers***. Bake
5 minutes until onions are golden.
Garnish with diced red bell
pepper, if desired.

Makes 6 servings

Tip: You may substitute 8 ounces
crumbled feta cheese for the
ricotta cheese. Omit salt.

Prep Time: 15 minutes
Cook Time: about 1 hour

Tidbit

*Ricotta is a type of
fresh cheese that is
somewhat lumpy, but
smoother than cottage
cheese. Since it's a fresh
cheese, it is highly perishable.
Make sure you're buying it
fresh.*

Mediterranean Strata

Wisconsin Swiss Linguine Tart

½ **cup butter, divided**
2 **cloves garlic, minced**
30 **thin French bread slices**
3 **tablespoons flour**
1 **teaspoon salt**
¼ **teaspoon white pepper**
    Dash nutmeg
2½ **cups milk**
¼ **cup grated Wisconsin**
    Parmesan cheese
2 **eggs, beaten**
2 **cups (8 ounces) shredded**
    Wisconsin Baby Swiss
    cheese, divided
8 **ounces fresh linguine,**
    cooked, drained
⅓ **cup green onion slices**
2 **tablespoons minced fresh**
    basil *or* 2 teaspoons dried
    basil, crushed
2 **plum tomatoes**

Melt ¼ cup butter. Add garlic; cook 1 minute. Brush 10-inch pie plate with butter mixture; line bottom and sides with bread, allowing bread to come 1 inch over sides. Brush bread with remaining butter mixture. Bake at 350°F for 5 minutes or until lightly browned. Set aside.

Melt remaining butter in saucepan over low heat. Blend in flour and seasonings. Gradually add milk; cook, stirring constantly, until thickened. Remove from heat; add Parmesan cheese. Stir small amount of sauce into eggs; mix well. Stir in remaining sauce.

Toss 1¼ cups Swiss cheese with linguine, green onions and basil. Pour sauce over linguine mixture; mix well. Pour into crust. Cut each tomato lengthwise into eight slices; place on tart. Sprinkle with remaining ¾ cup Swiss cheese. Bake at 350°F for 25 minutes or until warm. Let stand 5 minutes.

Makes 8 servings

Favorite recipe from ***Wisconsin Milk Marketing Board***

Tidbit

Pasta should be slightly undercooked when it is mixed with other ingredients in a casserole. It will continue to cook once it's in the oven.

Wisconsin Swiss Linguine Tart

Italian Eggplant Parmigiana

1 large eggplant, sliced ¼ inch thick
2 eggs, beaten
½ cup dry bread crumbs
1 can (14½ ounces) DEL MONTE® Italian Recipe Stewed Tomatoes
1 can (15 ounces) DEL MONTE® Tomato Sauce
2 cloves garlic, minced
½ teaspoon dried basil
6 ounces mozzarella cheese, sliced

1. Dip eggplant slices into eggs, then bread crumbs; arrange in single layer on baking sheet. Broil 4 inches from heat until brown and tender, about 5 minutes per side.

2. *Reduce oven temperature to 350°F.* Place eggplant in 13×9-inch baking dish.

3. Combine tomatoes, tomato sauce, garlic and basil; pour over eggplant and top with cheese.

4. Cover and bake at 350°F, 30 minutes or until heated through. Sprinkle with grated Parmesan cheese, if desired.
Makes 4 servings

Prep Time: 15 minutes
Cook Time: 30 minutes

Chili Relleno Casserole

1½ cups (6 ounces) SARGENTO® Light 4 Cheese Mexican Shredded Cheese or SARGENTO® Light Shredded Cheese for Tacos, divided
1 can (12 ounces) evaporated skim milk
¾ cup (6 ounces) fat-free liquid egg substitute or 3 eggs, beaten
6 (7-inch) corn tortillas, torn into 2-inch pieces
2 cans (4 ounces each) chopped green chilies
½ cup mild chunky salsa
¼ teaspoon salt (optional)
2 tablespoons chopped fresh cilantro
Light or fat-free sour cream (optional)

1. Coat 10-inch deep dish pie plate or 8-inch square baking dish with nonstick cooking spray. In medium bowl, combine 1 cup cheese, milk, egg substitute, tortillas, chilies, salsa and salt, if desired. Mix well; pour into prepared dish.

2. Bake at 375°F 30 to 32 minutes or until set. Remove from oven; sprinkle with remaining ½ cup cheese and cilantro. Return to oven; bake 1 minute or until cheese is melted. Serve with sour cream, if desired.
Makes 4 servings

Classic Stuffed Shells

1 jar (26 to 28 ounces) RAGÚ®
   Old World Style® Pasta
   Sauce, divided
2 pounds part-skim ricotta
   cheese
2 cups part-skim shredded
   mozzarella cheese
   (about 8 ounces)
¼ cup grated Parmesan cheese
3 eggs
1 tablespoon finely chopped
   fresh parsley
⅛ teaspoon ground black pepper
1 box (12 ounces) jumbo shells
   pasta, cooked and drained

Preheat oven to 350°F. In
13×9-inch baking pan, evenly
spread 1 cup Ragú® Old World
Style Pasta Sauce; set aside.

In large bowl, combine cheeses,
eggs, parsley and black pepper.
Fill shells with cheese mixture,
then arrange in baking pan. Evenly
top with remaining sauce. Bake
45 minutes or until sauce is
bubbling.   *Makes 8 servings*

Recipe Tip: For a change of shape,
substitute cooked and drained
cannelloni or manicotti tubes for
the jumbo shells. Use a teaspoon
or pastry bag to fill the tubes from
end to end, being careful not to
overfill them.

Cannellini Parmesan Casserole

2 tablespoons olive oil
1 cup chopped onion
2 teaspoons minced garlic
1 teaspoon dried oregano
   leaves
¼ teaspoon black pepper
2 cans (14½ ounces each)
   onion- and garlic-flavored
   diced tomatoes, undrained
1 jar (14 ounces) roasted red
   peppers, drained and cut
   into ½-inch squares
2 cans (19 ounces each) white
   cannellini beans or Great
   Northern beans, rinsed
   and drained
1 teaspoon dried basil leaves
   or 1 tablespoon chopped
   fresh basil
¾ cup (3 ounces) grated
   Parmesan cheese

1. Heat oil in Dutch oven over
medium heat until hot. Add onion,
garlic, oregano and pepper; cook
and stir 5 minutes or until onion is
tender.

2. Increase heat to high. Add
tomatoes with juice and red
peppers; cover and bring to a boil.

3. Reduce heat to medium. Stir
in beans; cover and simmer
5 minutes, stirring occasionally.
Stir in basil and sprinkle with
cheese.   *Makes 6 servings*

Prep and Cook Time: 20 minutes

Eggplant Crêpes with Roasted Tomato Sauce

**Roasted Tomato Sauce
(recipe follows)
2 eggplants (about 8 to 9 inches
 long), cut lengthwise into
 18 (¼-inch-thick) slices
Nonstick olive oil cooking
 spray
1 package (10 ounces) frozen
 chopped spinach, thawed
 and pressed dry
1 cup ricotta cheese
½ cup grated Parmesan cheese
1¼ cups (5 ounces) shredded
 Gruyère* cheese
Fresh oregano leaves for
 garnish**

*Gruyère cheese is a Swiss cheese that has been aged for 10 to 12 months. Any Swiss cheese may be substituted.

1. Preheat oven to 425°F. Prepare Roasted Tomato Sauce.

2. Arrange eggplant on nonstick baking sheets in single layer. Spray both sides of eggplant slices with cooking spray. Bake eggplant 10 minutes; turn and bake 5 to 10 minutes more or until tender. Cool. *Reduce oven temperature to 350°F.*

3. Combine spinach, ricotta and Parmesan cheese; mix well. Spray 12×8-inch baking pan with cooking spray. Spread spinach mixture evenly onto eggplant slices; roll up slices, beginning at short ends. Place rolls, seam sides down, in baking dish.

4. Cover dish with foil. Bake 25 minutes. Uncover; sprinkle rolls with Gruyère cheese. Bake, uncovered, 5 minutes more or until cheese is melted.

5. Serve with Roasted Tomato Sauce. Garnish, if desired.

Makes 4 to 6 servings

Roasted Tomato Sauce

**20 ripe plum tomatoes (about
 2⅔ pounds), cut into
 halves and seeded
3 tablespoons olive oil, divided
½ teaspoon salt
⅓ cup minced fresh basil
½ teaspoon black pepper**

Toss tomatoes with 1 tablespoon oil and salt. Place cut sides down on nonstick baking sheet. Bake 20 to 25 minutes or until skins are blistered. Cool. Process tomatoes, remaining 2 tablespoons oil, basil and pepper in food processor until smooth.   *Makes about 1 cup*

Eggplant Crêpes with Roasted Tomato Sauce

Ravioli with Homemade Tomato Sauce

3 cloves garlic, peeled
½ cup fresh basil leaves
3 cups seeded, peeled tomatoes, cut into quarters
2 tablespoons tomato paste
2 tablespoons commercial fat-free Italian salad dressing
1 tablespoon balsamic vinegar
¼ teaspoon black pepper
1 package (9 ounces) refrigerated reduced-fat cheese ravioli
2 cups shredded spinach leaves
1 cup (4 ounces) shredded part-skim mozzarella cheese

MICROWAVE DIRECTIONS

1. To prepare tomato sauce, process garlic in food processor until coarsely chopped. Add basil; process until coarsely chopped. Add tomatoes, tomato paste, salad dressing, vinegar and pepper; process, using on/off pulsing action, until tomatoes are chopped.

2. Spray 9-inch square microwavable dish with nonstick cooking spray. Spread 1 cup tomato sauce in dish. Layer half of ravioli and spinach over tomato sauce. Repeat layers with 1 cup tomato sauce and remaining ravioli and spinach. Top with remaining 1 cup of tomato sauce.

3. Cover with plastic wrap; refrigerate 1 to 8 hours. Vent plastic wrap. Microwave at MEDIUM (50% power) 20 minutes or until pasta is tender and hot. Sprinkle with cheese. Microwave at HIGH 3 minutes or just until cheese melts. Let stand, covered, 5 minutes before serving. Garnish, if desired. *Makes 6 servings*

Tidbit

Balsamic vinegar is an Italian aged vinegar with a distinctive mellow flavor. Its dark brown color is derived from the barrels in which it is aged. Look for it in the imported section of a supermarket or in a specialty food shop.

Ravioli with Homemade Tomato Sauce

Eggplant Squash Bake

½ **cup chopped onion**
1 **clove garlic, minced**
　　Nonstick olive oil cooking
　　spray
1 **cup part-skim ricotta cheese**
1 **jar (4 ounces) diced**
　　pimiento, drained
¼ **cup grated Parmesan cheese**
2 **tablespoons milk**
1½ **teaspoons dried marjoram**
¾ **teaspoon dried tarragon**
¼ **teaspoon salt**
¼ **teaspoon ground nutmeg**
¼ **teaspoon black pepper**
1 **cup no-sugar-added meatless**
　　spaghetti sauce, divided
½ **pound eggplant, peeled and**
　　cut into thin crosswise
　　slices
6 **ounces zucchini, cut in half,**
　　then lengthwise into thin
　　slices
6 **ounces yellow summer**
　　squash, cut in half, then
　　lengthwise into thin slices
2 **tablespoons shredded**
　　part-skim mozzarella
　　cheese

1. Combine onion and garlic in medium microwavable bowl. Spray lightly with cooking spray. Microwave at HIGH 1 minute.

2. Add ricotta, pimiento, Parmesan, milk, marjoram, tarragon, salt, nutmeg and pepper.

3. Spray 9- or 10-inch round microwavable baking dish with cooking spray. Spread ⅓ cup spaghetti sauce onto bottom of dish. Layer half of eggplant, zucchini and summer squash in dish; spoon on ricotta cheese mixture. Repeat layering with remaining eggplant, zucchini and summer squash. Top with remaining ⅔ cup spaghetti sauce.

4. Cover with vented plastic wrap. Microwave at HIGH 17 to 19 minutes or until vegetables are tender, rotating dish every 6 minutes. Top with mozzarella cheese. Let stand 10 minutes before serving.　　*Makes 4 servings*

Tidbit

Eggplant comes in a variety of shapes, colors and sizes. Look for a firm eggplant that is heavy for its size. It should have a tight, glossy, deeply-colored skin. The stem should be bright green. Dull skin and rust-colored spots are signs of old age.

Eggplant Squash Bake

Dishy Sides

pg. 80

pg. 88

1-2-3 Cheddar Broccoli Casserole

1 jar (16 ounces) RAGÚ® Cheese Creations!® Double Cheddar Sauce
2 boxes (10 ounces each) frozen broccoli florets, thawed
¼ cup plain or Italian seasoned dry bread crumbs
1 tablespoon margarine or butter, melted

1. Preheat oven to 350°F. In 1½-quart casserole, combine Ragú Cheese Creations! Sauce and broccoli.

2. Evenly top with bread crumbs combined with margarine.

3. Bake uncovered 20 minutes or until bread crumbs are golden and broccoli is tender.

Makes 6 servings

Tip: Substitute your favorite frozen vegetables for broccoli florets.

Prep Time: 5 minutes
Cook Time: 20 minutes

1-2-3 Cheddar Broccoli Casserole

Roasted Red Pepper & Tomato Casserole

1 jar (12 ounces) roasted red
   peppers, drained
1½ teaspoons red wine vinegar
1 teaspoon olive oil
1 clove garlic, minced
¼ teaspoon salt
¼ teaspoon black pepper
⅓ cup grated Parmesan cheese,
   divided
3 medium tomatoes (about
   1½ pounds), sliced
½ cup (about 1 ounce)
   herb-flavored croutons,
   crushed

1. Combine red peppers, vinegar, oil, garlic, salt and black pepper in food processor; process, using on/off pulsing action, 1 minute or until slightly chunky. Reserve 2 tablespoons cheese for garnish. Stir remaining cheese into red pepper mixture.

2. Arrange tomato slices in 8-inch round microwavable baking dish; microwave at HIGH 1 minute. Spoon red pepper mixture on top; microwave at HIGH 2 to 3 minutes or until tomatoes are slightly soft.

3. Sprinkle with reserved cheese and croutons. Garnish, if desired.
Makes 6 servings

Sweet Potato Crisp

1 can (40 ounces) cut sweet
   potatoes, drained
1 package (8 ounces)
   PHILADELPHIA® Cream
   Cheese, softened
¾ cup firmly packed brown
   sugar, divided
¼ teaspoon ground cinnamon
1 cup chopped apples
⅔ cup chopped cranberries
½ cup flour
½ cup old-fashioned or
   quick-cooking oats,
   uncooked
⅓ cup butter or margarine
¼ cup chopped pecans

MIX sweet potatoes, cream cheese, ¼ cup of the sugar and cinnamon with electric mixer on medium speed until well blended. Spoon into 1½-quart casserole or 10×6-inch baking dish. Top with apples and cranberries.

MIX flour, oats and remaining ½ cup sugar in medium bowl; cut in butter until mixture resembles coarse crumbs. Stir in pecans. Sprinkle over fruit.

BAKE at 350°F for 35 to 40 minutes or until thoroughly heated.
Makes 8 servings

Prep: 20 minutes
Bake: 40 minutes

Roasted Red Pepper & Tomato Casserole

Potatoes Au Gratin

4 to 6 medium unpeeled
    baking potatoes (about
    2 pounds)
2 cups (8 ounces) shredded
    Cheddar cheese
1 cup (4 ounces) shredded
    Swiss cheese
2 tablespoons butter or
    margarine
3 tablespoons all-purpose flour
2½ cups milk
2 tablespoons Dijon mustard
¼ teaspoon salt
¼ teaspoon black pepper

1. Preheat oven to 400°F. Grease
13×9-inch baking dish.

2. Cut potatoes into thin slices.
Layer potatoes in prepared dish.
Top with cheeses.

3. Melt butter in medium
saucepan over medium heat. Stir
in flour; cook 1 minute. Stir in
milk, mustard, salt and pepper;
bring to a boil. Reduce heat and
cook, stirring constantly, until
mixture thickens. Pour milk
mixture over cheese.

4. Cover pan with foil. Bake
30 minutes. Remove foil and bake
15 to 20 minutes more or until
potatoes are tender and top is
brown. Remove from oven and let
stand 10 minutes before serving.
Garnish, if desired.

Makes 6 to 8 servings

Zucchini al Forno

1 tablespoon olive oil
3 small zucchini (1 pound),
    thinly sliced
1 package (12 ounces)
    mushrooms, wiped clean
    and thinly sliced
1 jar (14 ounces) marinara
    sauce
1⅓ cups *French's®* *Taste*
    Toppers™ French Fried
    Onions, divided
½ cup ricotta cheese
⅓ cup grated Parmesan cheese
¼ cup milk
1 egg

Preheat oven to 375°F. Grease
2-quart oblong baking dish. Heat
oil in large nonstick skillet. Add
zucchini and mushrooms; cook
and stir about 3 minutes or until
crisp-tender. Stir in marinara sauce
and ⅔ cup **Taste Toppers**. Pour
into prepared baking dish.

Combine cheeses, milk and egg in
medium bowl; mix until well
blended. Spread cheese mixture
over vegetable mixture.

Bake, uncovered, 30 minutes or
until cheese layer is set. Sprinkle
with remaining ⅔ cup **Taste**
Toppers. Bake 3 minutes or until
Taste Toppers are golden.

Makes 4 to 6 servings

Prep Time: 15 minutes
Cook Time: 36 minutes

Potatoes Au Gratin

French's® Original Green Bean Casserole

1 can (10¾ ounces) condensed cream of mushroom soup
¾ cup milk
⅛ teaspoon pepper
2 packages (9 ounces each) frozen cut green beans, thawed*
1⅓ cups *French's*® Taste Toppers™ French Fried Onions, divided

*Substitute 2 cans (14½ ounces each) cut green beans, drained, for frozen green beans.

1. Preheat oven to 350°F. Combine soup, milk and pepper in 1½-quart casserole; stir until well blended. Stir in beans and ⅔ cup **Taste Toppers**.

2. Bake, uncovered, 30 minutes or until hot; stir. Sprinkle with remaining ⅔ cup **Taste Toppers**. Bake 5 minutes or until **Taste Toppers** are golden brown.

Makes 6 servings

Microwave Directions: Prepare green bean mixture as above; pour into 1½-quart microwave-safe casserole. Cover with vented plastic wrap. Microwave on HIGH 8 to 10 minutes or until heated through, stirring halfway. Uncover. Top with remaining **Taste Toppers**. Cook 1 minute until **Taste Toppers** are golden. Let stand 5 minutes.

Substitution: You may substitute 4 cups cooked, cut fresh green beans for the frozen or canned.

Prep Time: 5 minutes
Cook Time: 35 minutes

Creamy Mac & Cheese Alfredo

8 ounces elbow macaroni, cooked and drained
1 jar (16 ounces) RAGÚ® Cheese Creations!® Classic Alfredo Sauce
¾ cup chicken broth
¼ cup plain dry bread crumbs
2 tablespoons grated Parmesan cheese (optional)

1. Preheat oven to 350°F. In large bowl, combine hot macaroni, Ragú Cheese Creations! Sauce and broth. Season, if desired, with salt and pepper.

2. In 1-quart baking dish, spoon macaroni mixture; sprinkle with bread crumbs and cheese. Bake uncovered 25 minutes or until heated through.

Makes 4 servings

Prep Time: 10 minutes
Cook Time: 25 minutes

Autumn Casserole

¼ cup fat-free reduced-sodium chicken broth or water
2 cups sliced mushrooms
2 cups washed, stemmed and chopped fresh spinach
1 cup diced red bell pepper
1 clove garlic, minced
1 cup cooked spaghetti squash
¼ teaspoon salt
¼ teaspoon black pepper
⅛ teaspoon dried Italian seasoning
⅛ teaspoon red pepper flakes (optional)
¼ cup grated Parmesan cheese

1. Preheat oven to 350°F. Spray 1-quart casserole with nonstick cooking spray.

2. Heat chicken broth in medium saucepan. Add mushrooms, spinach, bell pepper and garlic. Cook 10 minutes or until vegetables are tender, stirring frequently. Stir in squash. Add salt, black pepper, Italian seasoning and red pepper flakes, if desired.

3. Spoon into prepared casserole. Sprinkle with cheese. Bake 5 to 10 minutes or until cheese melts.

Makes 6 (½-cup) servings

Note: For 1 cup cooked spaghetti squash, place ½ spaghetti squash in microwavable dish and add ¼ cup water. Microwave at HIGH 8 to 10 minutes or until squash is tender when pierced with a fork. Discard seeds and scrape out strands of squash.

Lemon Rice Pilaf

1 onion, minced
¼ cup FLEISCHMANN'S® Original Margarine, divided
2 cups long-grain rice, uncooked
2 (14½-ounce) cans chicken broth
2 tablespoons lemon juice
2 teaspoons grated lemon peel
1 bay leaf
   Salt and freshly ground black pepper, to taste
2 tablespoons minced fresh parsley or 2 teaspoons dried parsley flakes
2 tablespoons pine nuts, toasted

1. Cook and stir onion in 3 tablespoons margarine in large saucepan over medium-high heat for 3 minutes. Add rice, stirring to coat well.

2. Add broth, lemon juice, lemon peel, bay leaf and salt and pepper to taste. Heat to a boil; reduce heat to low. Cover; cook for 15 to 20 minutes or until liquid is absorbed. Remove from heat; let stand 5 minutes.

3. Mix remaining 1 tablespoon margarine, parsley and pine nuts into rice. Serve immediately.

Makes 4 to 6 servings

Preparation Time: 10 minutes
Cook Time: 25 minutes
Total Time: 35 minutes

Wild Rice Mushroom Stuffing

½ cup uncooked wild rice
    Day-old French bread (about
    4 ounces)
½ cup butter or margarine
1 large onion, chopped
1 clove garlic, minced
3 cups sliced fresh
    mushrooms*
½ teaspoon rubbed sage
½ teaspoon dried thyme leaves,
    crushed
½ teaspoon salt
¼ teaspoon black pepper
1 cup chicken broth
½ cup coarsely chopped pecans
    Thyme sprigs for garnish

*Or, substitute 1½ cups sliced fresh shiitake mushrooms for 1½ cups of the fresh mushrooms.

Rinse and cook rice according to package directions; set aside.

Cut enough bread into ½-inch cubes to measure 4 cups. Spread in single layer on baking sheet. Broil 5 to 6 inches from heat 4 minutes or until lightly toasted, stirring after 2 minutes; set aside.

Melt butter in large skillet over medium heat. Add onion and garlic. Cook and stir 3 minutes. Add mushrooms; cook 3 minutes, stirring occasionally. Add sage, dried thyme leaves, salt and pepper. Add cooked rice; cook 2 minutes, stirring occasionally. Stir in broth. Add pecans and toasted bread cubes; toss lightly.

Transfer to 1½-quart casserole.** Preheat oven to 325°F. Cover casserole with lid or foil. Bake 40 minutes or until heated through. Garnish with thyme sprigs, if desired.

Makes 6 to 8 servings

**At this point, Wild Rice Mushroom Stuffing may be covered and refrigerated up to 8 hours before baking. Bake 50 minutes or until heated through.

Hash Brown Bake

1 packet (1 ounce) HIDDEN
    VALLEY® Original Ranch®
    Dressing Mix
1¼ cups milk
3 ounces cream cheese
6 cups hash browns, frozen
    shredded potatoes
1 tablespoon bacon bits
½ cup shredded Sharp Cheddar
    cheese

In blender, combine dressing mix, milk and cream cheese. Pour over potatoes and bacon bits in 9-inch baking dish. Top with cheese. Bake at 350°F for 35 minutes.

Makes 4 servings

Wild Rice Mushroom Stuffing

Apple-Rice Medley

- 1 package (6 ounces) long-grain and wild rice mix
- 1 cup (4 ounces) shredded mild Cheddar cheese, divided
- 1 cup chopped Washington Golden Delicious apple
- 1 cup sliced mushrooms
- ½ cup thinly sliced celery

Prepare rice mix according to package directions. Preheat oven to 350°F. Add ½ cup cheese, apple, mushrooms and celery to rice; toss to combine. Spoon mixture into 1-quart casserole dish. Bake 15 minutes. Top with remaining ½ cup cheese; bake until cheese melts, about 10 minutes.   *Makes 4 servings*

MICROWAVE DIRECTIONS

Combine cooked rice, ½ cup cheese, apple, mushrooms and celery as directed; spoon mixture into 1-quart microwave-safe dish. Microwave at HIGH 3 to 4 minutes or until heated through. Top with remaining ½ cup cheese; microwave at HIGH 1 minute or until cheese melts.

Favorite recipe from **Washington Apple Commission**

Crunchy Onion Stuffing

- 1 package (8 ounces) herb-seasoned stuffing
- 1⅓ cups *French's® Taste Toppers™* French Fried Onions, divided
- ½ cup finely chopped celery
- ½ cup finely chopped carrots
- 1 can (14½ ounces) reduced-sodium chicken broth
- 1 egg, beaten

Combine stuffing, ⅔ cup **Taste Toppers** and vegetables in 2-quart microwavable shallow casserole. Mix broth and egg in small bowl; pour over stuffing. Stir to coat evenly. Cover; microwave on HIGH 10 minutes* or until vegetables are tender, stirring halfway through cooking time. Sprinkle with remaining ⅔ cup **Taste Toppers**. Microwave 1 minute or until **Taste Toppers** are golden.   *Makes 6 servings*

*Or bake, covered, in preheated 350°F oven 40 to 45 minutes.

Tip: For a moister stuffing, add up to ½ cup water to chicken broth. You may add ½ cup cooked sausage or 2 tablespoons crumbled, cooked bacon to stuffing, if desired.

Prep Time: 10 minutes
Cook Time: 11 minutes

Apple-Rice Medley

Vegetable Parmesan Bake

1 envelope LIPTON® RECIPE
    SECRETS® Garlic
    Mushroom Soup Mix
¼ cup grated Parmesan cheese
1 large baking potato, cut into
    ¼-inch-thick slices
1 medium zucchini, diagonally
    cut into ¼-inch-thick slices
1 large tomato, cut into
    ¼-inch-thick slices
1 tablespoon margarine or
    butter, cut into small
    pieces

1. Preheat oven to 375°F. In small bowl, combine soup mix and Parmesan cheese; set aside.

2. In shallow 1-quart casserole sprayed with nonstick cooking spray, arrange potato slices, overlapping slightly. Sprinkle with ⅓ of the soup mixture. Top with zucchini slices, overlapping slightly. Sprinkle with ⅓ of the soup mixture. Top with tomato slices, overlapping slightly. Sprinkle with remaining soup mixture. Top with margarine.

3. Bake covered 40 minutes. Remove cover and bake an additional 10 minutes or until vegetables are tender.

Makes 4 servings

SPAM™ Corn Pudding

1 (12-ounce) can SPAM®
    Luncheon Meat, cubed
⅓ cup chopped green bell
    pepper
¼ cup chopped onion
2 tablespoons butter or
    margarine
6 eggs
2 cups milk
1 tablespoon all-purpose flour
2 teaspoons sugar
1 teaspoon salt
⅛ teaspoon black pepper
2 (10-ounce) packages frozen
    whole kernel corn, thawed
    and drained

Heat oven to 300°F. In large skillet, sauté SPAM®, bell pepper and onion in butter until tender. In large bowl, beat eggs. Stir in milk, flour, sugar, salt and black pepper. Add SPAM™ mixture and corn. Pour into greased 12×8-inch baking dish. Bake 1 hour and 10 minutes or until set.

Makes 8 servings

Vegetable Parmesan Bake

Acknowledgments

**The publisher would like to thank the companies
and organizations listed below for the use of their recipes and
photographs in this publication.**

American Lamb Council

BelGioioso® Cheese, Inc.

Bob Evans®

Butterball® Turkey Company

Del Monte Corporation

Filippo Berio® Olive Oil

Fleischmann's® Original Spread

Florida Department of
Agriculture and Consumer
Services, Bureau of Seafood
and Aquaculture

The Golden Grain Company®

Hillshire Farm®

Hormel Foods, LLC

The HV Company

The J.M. Smucker Company

Kraft Foods Holdings

Lawry's® Foods, Inc.

National Turkey Federation

Nestlé USA, Inc.

Newman's Own, Inc.®

Perdue Farms Incorporated

Reckitt Benckiser

Sargento® Foods Inc.

Unilever Bestfoods North
America

USA Rice Federation

Washington Apple
Commission

Wisconsin Milk Marketing
Board

Index